CogAT © Practice Test (Grade 7 and 8)

Includes Tips for preparing for the CogAT© Test

Authored, written by : Bright Minds Publishing, Seattle WA

Bright Minds Publishing
Seattle, WA

Contents

Introduction to CogAT©

Introduction

The Cognitive Abilities Test (CogAT©, CAT) is a K–12 assessment designed to measure students' learned reasoning abilities in the three areas most linked to academic success in school:

1. Verbal
2. Quantitative
3. Nonverbal

Although its primary goal is to assess students' reasoning abilities, CogAT© can also provide predicted achievement scores when administered with the Iowa Tests.

CogAT© is also often used to help educators make student placement decisions, especially when selecting students for Gifted and Talented programs.

Each level of CogAT© offers test batteries in the three aforementioned categories. CogAT© can be administered in whole or in part; however, the most complete view of a student will be provided through administration of all three batteries.

Structure of CogAT©

The CogAT© test consists of the following 9 sections - 3 each in Verbal, Quantitative and NonVerbal skills. Each test has a certain time allocated to finish the questions.

Section Name	Number of Questions	Minutes
Verbal Battery		
Section1: Verbal Classification	20	13
Section 2: Sentence Completion	20	13
Section 3: Verbal Analogies	25	13
Quantitative Battery		
Section 4: Quantitative Relations	25	12
Section 5: Number Series	20	13
Section 6: Equation Building	15	15
Non Verbal Battery		
Section 7: Figure Classification	25	13
Section 8: Figure Analogies	25	13
Section 9: Figure Analysis	15	13
Total	190	

Tips to prepare for CogAT©

I.   Understand the structure of the test: Take time to understand what skill is tested in each section. This will give you an edge over other test takers since it will save time understanding what is expected from you in the time bound test.

II. Start planning early so that you can take a practice test, time it and figure out your problem areas. Once you know your problem areas, solve multiple problems in that area of weakness (if any).

III. Test section specific Tips

1. Verbal Classification: Figure out the general "theme" or "class" for the various words mentioned in the problems. It can be a verb, noun, name, place, thing or some attribute of name, place, item or thing.

2. Sentence Completion: Figure out which word completes the sentence that sounds correct from a grammatical and punctuation perspective. Test taker's vocabulary plays an important role in scoring well in this section.

3. Verbal Analogies: Analogies can be synonyms, antonyms, cause and effect, general and specific, classification and specific, degree of intensity or part or whole. Try to figure out what is the "theme" of the analogy.

4. Quantitative Relations: Master fundamentals of fractions, measurements, decimals and other basic arithmetic operations like additions, subtraction, multiplication and division without a calculator.

5. Number Series: Figure out the patterns involved in the series, they can be derived by checking for additions, subtractions, division and multiplication, specific property of numbers etc.

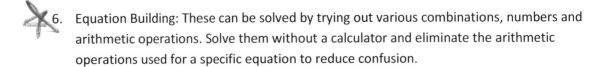

6. Equation Building: These can be solved by trying out various combinations, numbers and arithmetic operations. Solve them without a calculator and eliminate the arithmetic operations used for a specific equation to reduce confusion.

7. Figure Classification: Identify the theme involved in the various figures and how they change. The change can be related to size, shape, number of sides, slicing the image,

rotating or mirror images. These can be done one at a time or multiple changes at one time.

8. Figure Analogies: Identify the theme involved in the various figures and how they change. The change can be related to size, shape, number of sides, slicing the image, rotating, mirror images or rotations. These can be done one at a time or multiple changes at one time.

9. Figure Analysis: Try working your way back from the completely folded image one step at a time as you unfold the piece of paper. During practice encourage the test taker to play with scraps of paper to get familiar with the concept of folding and unfolding and watching how the size and shape changes with each fold and punched hole.

IV. Get familiar with marking the bubbles in the answer sheet. Ensure you cover the entire bubble since the answer sheets are machine scanned and partially filled bubbles may be misread by the machine reader.

V. If you skip any question, ensure that you don't mark incorrect bubbles for subsequent questions on the test. Always call out the question number you are solving and the bubble you are marking in your head when you are ready to mark the bubble on your answer sheet.

VI. Remember the acronym RTMC – which stands for Read, Think, Mark and Check.

- Read: Always read the question in its entirety for what it is asking for. Even if you have seen this question before, chances are that the test question may be asking you to deduce something different.
- Think: Think before you answer.
- Mark: Mark the correct bubble on your answer sheet.
- Check: Always check your answers when you finish all the questions before the time for a section is up.

Section 1: Verbal Classification

Instructions:

Here is a sample question in this section:

Bird	Cat	Fish	?
A. Dog	B. Tiger	C. Lion	D. Bear

Read the question. The first three words belong to a specific category. Now read all the 4 options and think about which one closely belongs to the same category of the three words. On the blank answer sheet at the end of this book, pencil in the bubble to answer the question.

The correct answer here is option A because it belongs to the category Pets like the first three words.

All the questions in this section can be solved in the same manner.

1. Cinematographer   Director   Producer   ?

A. Actor   B. Villain   C. Choreographer   D. Drama

2. Planning   Designing   Coding   ?

A. Computer   B. Debugging   C. Software   D. Virus

3. Thyme   Dill   Mint   ?

A. Soup   B. Curry   C. Spices   D. Cilantro

4. Basketball   Rugby   Hockey   ?

A. Professional   B. Lacrosse   C. College   D. Championship

5. Symphony   Ballet   Theater   ?

A. Opera   B. Stage   C. Audience   D. Entertainment

6. Roast   Bake   Fry   ?

A. Sauté   B. Food   C. Hungry   D. Chicken

7. Hound   Sheppard   Retriever   ?

A. Dog   B. Peasant   C. Terrier   D. Pet

8. Christianity   Muslim   Buddhism   ?

A. Moon   B. Christ   C. Hinduism   D. Prayers

9.   Earth   Wind   Fire   ?

A. Dry   B. Hot   C. Cold   D. Water

10.   Strawberries   Cranberries   Mulberries   ?

A. Blackcurrants   B. Smoothie   C. Juice   D. Sweet

11.   Fettuccine   Fusilli   Lasagna   ?

A. Tomato   B. Orzo   C. Sauce   D. Meatballs

12.   Frustration   Angry   Worry   ?

A. Annoyed   B. Happy   C. Ecstatic   D. Excited

13.   Pyramids   Coliseum   Great-Wall   ?

A. Tourists   B. Stonehenge   C. Lake   D. Wonders

14.   Picasso   Monet   Van Gogh   ?

A. Mona Lisa   B. Water-lilies   C. Degas   D. Oil Paintings

15.   Roosevelt   Ford   Clinton   ?

A. Truman   B. Politician   C. Washington DC   D. President

16.   Custard   Pudding   Pies   ?

A. Sweet   B. Cake   C. Apple   D. Pumpkin

17. Corn flakes   wheat-thins   Raisin-bran   ?

A. Morning   B. Cereal   C. Granola   D. Energy

18. Verb   Noun   Adverb   ?

A. Grammar   B. English   C. Adjective   D. Poem

19. Decline   Drop   Deteriorate   ?

A. Depreciate   B. Zero   C. Half   D. Increase

20. Roses   Dahlia   Hydrangea   ?

A. Fragrance   B. Bouquet   C. Valentine   D. Lilies

Section 2: Sentence Completion

Instructions:

Here is a sample question in this section:

The 4th grade students were _____ to have Mr. Anderson as their 5th Grade teacher next year since he was known to be an awesome teacher, motivator and cared a lot for his students.

A. frustrated   B. delighted   C. hungry   D. sleepy

Read the sentence. Then read the word options A through D. Try and figure out which of these words when substituted for the blank space in the sentence makes the sentence complete and correct. On the blank answer sheet at the end of this book, pencil in the bubble the answer for the question.

The correct answer here is option B because it describes a mood reflected by students when they heard that Mr. Anderson would be their class teacher in 5th Grade.

All the questions in this section can be solved in the same manner.

1. The children had an amazing _____ for their school play this last week where everyone remembered their roles, dialogues and cues.
    A. rehearsal
    B. break
    C. audience
    D. stage

2. The doctor recommended that Irene take _____ and ample rest for a couple of days to recover from the influenza symptoms that were bothering her.
    A. classes
    B. medication
    C. showers
    D. exercise

3. The teacher holds the children to a high _____ for all the assignments and homework and this has helped them improve the quality of their learning and work.
    A. bar
    B. volume
    C. timeliness
    D. place

4. The internet has _____ how businesses market & sell their products online by improving the speed of communication.
    A. online
    B. transformed
    C. initiated
    D. computers

5. Percy got admitted to University of California, LA on a football _____ and this helped him advance him learning, pay for tuition and advance him football skills.
    A. players
    B. scholarship
    C. ground
    D. program

6. The winter blizzard practically _____ all air and road traffic coming into an out of Washington DC area for several days.
    A. improved
    B. cleared
    C. paralyzed
    D. decreased

7. The police are still investigating the _____ in crime in the Bradford county which has caused the locals to step up vigilance in local communities.
    A. decline
    B. elimination
    C. popularity
    D. surge

8. The counselor spent time talking to members about their _____ and aspirations at the public meeting and offered practical and useful solutions.
    A. challenges
    B. victories
    C. finances
    D. health

9. The _____ of the camera has provided a mechanism for capturing the details of an image and hence helped capture moments that can be shared with others at a later date.
    A. job
    B. art
    C. decline
    D. invention

10. Mass manufacturing of affordable automobiles was debuted by Ransom Olds at his Oldsmobile factory in 1902 based on the _____ line techniques pioneered by Marc Isambard Brunel at the Portsmouth Block Mills, England in 1802.
    A. straight
    B. assembly
    C. transport
    D. product

11. The Louvre museum is one of the largest, most visited museum in the world hold nearly 35,000 objects from _____ to 19th century.

A. prehistoric
B. modern
C. fragile
D. cast-iron

12. _____ work at the Anyang, which has been identified as the last Shang capital, uncovered eleven major Yin royal tombs and the foundations of palaces used by the royals in the Shang dynasty.

   A. Digging
   B. Mechanical
   C. Archeological
   D. Mason

13. Muir Woods national monument was established to protect an old-growth coast from _____ and provides visitors with excellent paved roads and easy access board walks.

   A. population
   B. township
   C. destruction
   D. growth

14. Studies have shown that apples and apple products (like sauce and juice) can help lower your risk of _____ heart disease and may also help decrease your waist size and possibly even your blood pressure.

   A. contracting
   B. developing
   C. increasing
   D. decreasing

15. The Internal Revenue Service (IRS) is responsible for collecting _____ and the interpretation and enforcement of monetary code.

   A. taxes
   B. wages
   C. receipts
   D. land

16. Pet Assisted Therapy is a new field of study that involves animals as a form of treatment to improve patient's _____, emotional and cognitive functions.

A. social

B. cultural

C. economical

D. artistic

17. Computer virus or worm is a computer _____ that uses computer network to send copies of itself to other computers on the network and may cause havoc by deleting files important to the user.

A. network

B. program

C. monitor

D. keyboard

18. Local roadways, despite showing signs of increasing _____ due to increasing population, are relatively easy to travel via a variety of means like public transport, bikes etc.

A. congestion

B. people

C. shops

D. trash

19. Law is a system of _____ and guidelines which are enforced through social institutions to govern behavior, wherever possible.

A. judges

B. rules

C. courts

D. meetings

20. Honey bees _____ nectar from flower into honey by a process of regurgitation, and store it as a primary food source in the wax honeycombs inside the beehive.

A. produce

B. search

C. combine

D. transform

Section 3: Verbal Analogies

Instructions:

Here is a sample question in this section:

Angry:: Happy   Sunny:: _____

A. Hot   B. Cloudy   C. drought   D. Floods

Read the analogy. Then read the word options A through D. Try and figure out the relationship between 1ˢᵗ word and 2ⁿᵈ word. Then figure out which of the options A through D has the same relationship with the 3ʳᵈ word. On the blank answer sheet at the end of this book, pencil in the bubble to answer the question.

The correct answer here is option B because the relationship between Angry and Happy are opposites. Only option B is an opposite of the word Sunny.

All the questions in this section can be solved in the same manner.

1. Dog :: Bark   People :: _____
A. Walk   B. Talk   C. Sing   D. Scold

2. School :: Fish   Herd :: _____
A. Antelope   B. Bats   C. Butterfly   D. Chicken

3. Refrigerator :: Cold   Oven :: _____
A. Hot   B. Cooking   C. Grill   D. Barbecue

4. Noodles :: Strand   Rice :: _____
A. Porridge   B. Morsel   C. White   D. Licorice

5. Camera :: Battery   People :: _____
A. Lunch   B. Breakfast   C. Food   D. Dinner

6. Telescope :: Planets   _____ :: Birds
A. Binoculars   B. Microscope C. Camera   D. Camcorder

7. Transparent :: See-through   Opaque:: _____
A. Shadow   B. Light   C. Impervious D. Lens

8. Cartoon :: Animation   Action :: _____
A. Stage-play   B. Drama   C. Hero   D. Villain

9. Gallon :: Quart   Hours :: _____
A. Morning   B. Watch   C. Clock   D. Minutes

10. Lemon :: Lemonade   Grape :: _____
A. Wine   B. Coke   C. Twist   D. Water

11. Clothes :: Laundry   Automobile :: _____
A. Car-wash   B. Vacuum   C. Glass-cleaner   D. Shampoo

12. Dictionary :: Words   Encyclopedia :: _____
A. Numbers   B. Information   C. Math   D. Science

13. Oncologist :: Cancer   Ophthalmologist :: _____
A. Vision   B. Ears   C. Nose   D. Teeth

14. Eyesight :: Blind   Sleep: _____
A. Awake   B. Insomnia   C. Bed   D. Carpet

15. Studio :: Music   Laboratory :: _____
A. Experiments   B. Reaction   C. Heater   D. Cooler

16. Coffee :: Caffeine   Hot-Chocolate:: _____
A. Sweet   B. Cocoa   C. Desert   D. Energy

17. Puppy:: Dog   Cub:: _____
A. Bear   B. Cow   C. Fox   D. Horse

18. Book :: Chapter   TV Series:: _____
A. Episodes   B. Actors   C. Themes   D. Genre

19. Larvae :: Butterfly   Tadpole:: _____
A. Worm   B. Frog   C. Moth   D. Insect

20. Amazing:: Astonishing Ridiculous:: _____
A. Humongous   B. Confusing   C. Complex   D. Absurd

21. Entertaining:: Amusing Boring:: _____
A. Lackluster   B. Slow   C. Tiring   D. No-theme

22. Milk :: Cheese   Beef :: _____
A. Chicken   B. Turkey   C. Jerky   D. Pork

23. Desk :: desktop computer   Portable:: _____
A. Keyboard   B. Mouse   C. Wireless   D. Laptop

24. Baseball:: Home run   Football::_____
A. Touch-down   B. Helmet   C. Super Bowl   D. Rose Bowl

25. Disgusting:: Repulsive   Attractive:: _____
A. Alluring   B. Mature   C. Unkempt   D. Boastful

Section 4: Quantitative Relations

Instructions:

Here is a sample question in this section:

I.   20% of 20
II.   50% of 10

    A. I is greater than II
    B. I is less than II
    C. I is equal to II

Read both the problems I and II. Solve these questions using mathematical formulas, concepts and rules you have learnt in your mathematics study. Figure out the relationship between problem I and Problem II. If the answer for problem I is greater than the answer for problem II choose A. If the answer for problem I is less than the answer for problem II then choose B. If the answer for problem I is equal to the answer for problem II then choose C. On the blank answer sheet at the end of this book, pencil in the bubble to answer the question.

The correct answer here is Option B because answer for I is 4 and answer for II is 5.

All the questions in this section can be solved in the same manner.

1. I. 150 x (1 ÷ 2)
   II. 100 x (3 ÷ 4)

   A. I is greater than II
   B. I is less than II
   C. I is equal to II

2. I. 2 Pints
   II. 1 Quart

   A. I is greater than II
   B. I is less than II
   C. I is equal to II

3. I. 2 x radius
   II. Diameter÷2

   A. I is greater than II
   B. I is less than II
   C. I is equal to II

4. I. 1 Litre
   II. 1 Gallon

   A. I is greater than II
   B. I is less than II
   C. I is equal to II

5. I. 7÷8
   II. ¾

   A. I is greater than II
   B. I is less than II
   C. I is equal to II

6. I. 11÷12
    II. 11÷9

    A. I is greater than II
    B. I is less than II
    C. I is equal to II

7. I. 5 ÷ 6
    II. 3 ÷ 6

    A. I is greater than II
    B. I is less than II
    C. I is equal to II

8. I. 1/8 x 1/8
    II 1/8 + 1/8
    A. I is greater than II
    B. I is less than II
    C. I is equal to II

9. I. P ÷ 2 = 24
    II. 135 ÷ Q = 45

    A. P is greater than Q
    B. P is less than Q
    C. P is equal to Q

10. I.   0.50000
    II.   5

    A. I is greater than II
    B. I is less than II
    C. I is equal to II

11. I. $2 \div 5 + ¾$

    II. ½ + 5/6

    A. I is greater than II

    B. I is less than II

    C. I is equal to II

12. I. 40% of 50

    II. 50% of 40

    A. I is greater than II

    B. I is less than II

    C. I is equal to II

13. I. 3^3

    II. 4^2

    A. I is greater than II

    B. I is less than II

    C. I is equal to II

14. I. Square root of (32 + 32)

    II. 6

    A. I is greater than II

    B. I is less than II

    C. I is equal to II

15. I. $1 \div X$

    II. X where X is positive whole number greater than 1

    A. I is greater than II

    B. I is less than II

    C. I is equal to II

16. I.   Area of a circle

II. Perimeter of a circle, where radius is greater than 2 cm

   A.   I is greater than II
   B.   I is less than II
   C.   I is equal to II

17. I. Sum of 2 sides of triangle

II. 3rd Side of the same triangle

   A.   I is greater than II
   B.   I is less than II
   C.   I is equal to II

18. I. 20% of 1 Dollar and 25 cents

II. One Quarter

   A.   I is greater than II
   B.   I is less than II
   C.   I is equal to II

19. I.   ¼ + 5/8
    II.   3/8 + ½

   A.   I is greater than II
   B.   I is less than II
   C.   I is equal to II

20. I. Number of pencils you can buy at 10 cents each for $2.50

II. Number of erasers you can buy for 5 cents each for $1.30

   A.   I is greater than II
   B.   I is less than II
   C.   I is equal to II

21. I. Product of 2 numbers
    II. Sum of 2 numbers, where both the numbers are whole numbers less than 0

    A. I is greater than II
    B. I is less than II
    C. I is equal to II

22. I. Price of apple when you get 15% off on price of 80 cents.
    II. Price of orange when you get 25% off on 84 cents.

    A. I is greater than II
    B. I is less than II
    C. I is equal to II

23. I. Probability of getting the side with one dot on the top of a regular dice roll
    II. Probability of getting the side with three dots on the top of a regular dice roll

    A. I is greater than II
    B. I is less than II
    C. I is equal to II

24. I. 0.6 x 0.6
    II. 0.6 ÷ 0.6

    A. I is greater than II
    B. I is less than II
    C. I is equal to II

25. I. Number of sides for Parallelogram
    II. Number of sides of a rectangle

    A. I is greater than II
    B. I is less than II
    C. I is equal to II

Section 5: Number Series

Instructions:

Here is a sample question in this section:

50   100   200   400   ?

A. 500   B.600   C.700   D.800

Read the number in the series. Figure out the relationship between these number and the pattern that ties all these numbers together. Once you figure that out, read the options A through D. Figure out which pattern fits best to be the next number in the series.

The correct answer here is option D because pattern here is that the number doubles each time and hence the next number in the series is 800.

All the questions in this section can be solved in the same manner.

1.   1   4   9   16   ?

A. 22
B. 25
C. 21
D. 36

2.   1   8   27   64   ?

A. 100
B. 99
C. 125
D. 156

3.   23   25   28   32   ?

  A. 37
  B. 36
  C. 38
  D. 39

4.   ¼   ½   1 ¼   2 ½   ?

  A. 4 ¾
  B. 4
  C. 4 ¼
  D. 1 ½

5.   60   72   84   96   ?

  A. 108
  B. 120
  C. 110
  D. 112

6.   1   2   3   5   7   11   13   ?

    A. 15
    B. 17
    C. 18
    D. 19

7.   0   1   3   6   10   15   ?

    A. 21
    B. 20
    C. 22
    D. 25

8.   2   6   24   120   ?

    A. 600
    B. 720
    C. 700
    D. 800

9.   1   4   16   64   256   ?

    A. 1024
    B. 512
    C. 2048
    D. 4096

10.   5   15   30   50   75   ?

    A. 100
    B. 105
    C. 110
    D. 115

11.   -0.18   -0.20   -0.25   -0.33   ?

A. -0.55
B. -0.50
C. -0.44
D. -0.56

12.   45   56   67   78   ?

A. 89
B. 90
C. 91
D. 87

13.   4   8   32   256   ?

A. 512
B. 1024
C. 2048
D. 4096

14.   13   17   22   28   ?

A. 34
B. 35
C. 36
D. 40

15.   0   0.11   0.23   0.36   ?

A. 0.49
B. 0.51
C. 0.50
D. 0.52

16.　　　1　　5　　14　　30　　??

A. 55
B. 56
C. 45
D. 46

17.　　　1　　2　　2　　4　　8　　32　　?

A. 256
B. 64
C. 128
D. 512

18.　　　1　　1　　2　　3　　5　　8　　?

A. 11
B. 12
C. 25
D. 13

19.　　　34　　51　　68　　85　　?

A. 102
B. 98
C. 103
D. 101

20.　　　1　　45　　104　　1034　　?

A. 34556
B. 4567
C. 401
D. 54

Section 6: Equation Building

Instructions:

Here is a sample question in this section:

10	5	2	x	-	(	)

A. 10   B.0   C.1   D.100

Read the numbers along with the mathematical operators. Figure out how these numbers when placed in a specific order along with the operations will give one of the options On the blank answer sheet at the end of this book, pencil in the bubble to answer the question.

The correct answer here is Option B because the equation here is (5 x 2) – 10 = 0.

All the questions in this section can be solved in the same manner.

1.   5   10   0.1   X   ÷

A. 2.1   B. 5   C. 50.1   15.1

2.   ½   ¾   ½   ½   X   +   +   (   )

A. ¾   B. 1   C. 1¼   D. 1

3.   1   ¼   3   +   X   (   )

A. 1   B. 0.5   C. 2   D.4

4.   5   2   ½   0.5   -   +   X   (   )

A. 3   B. 5   C. 4   D. 6

5.   6   9   5   5   +   -   X   (   )

A. 54   B. 50   C. 55   D. 56

6.   16   9   √   +   (   )

A. 25   B. 5   C. 3   D. 4

7.   ¾   10   0.5   X   -   (   )

A. 8   B. 7   C. 2   D. 5

8.   5   5   5   1   x   ÷   ÷

A. 0.25   B. 0.5   C. 0.2   D. 1

9.   0.1   0.01   100   +   x   (   )

A. 1.1   B. 0.1   C. 0.11   D. 1.01

10.   4   5   6   8   +   -   x   (   )

A. 10   B. 15   C. 20   D. 18

11.   4   4   4   12   -   x   ÷   (   )

A. 2   B. 1   C. 0.5   D. 10

12.   5   10   15   20   ÷   ÷   x

A. 6   B. 9   C. 12   D.8

13.   2   4   8   16   x   x   ÷

A. 2   B. 4   C. 6   D. 8

14.   625   25   5   1   x   ÷   ÷

A. 1   B. 100   C. 25   D. 5

15.   1   1   1   1   +   ÷   x   (   )

A. 0   B. 1   C. 2   D. 3

Section 7: Figure Classifications

Instructions:

Here is a sample question in this section:

A	B	C	D

See the first three figures and out the relationship between these figures. Then see Answers A through D. See which option would be the next figure in the series to fit in the relationship you found earlier. On the blank answer sheet at the end of this book, pencil in the bubble the answer for the question.

The correct answer here is option A because the relationship between first three figures is that the figure is rotated by 90 degrees clock wise each time.

All the questions in this section can be solved in the same manner.

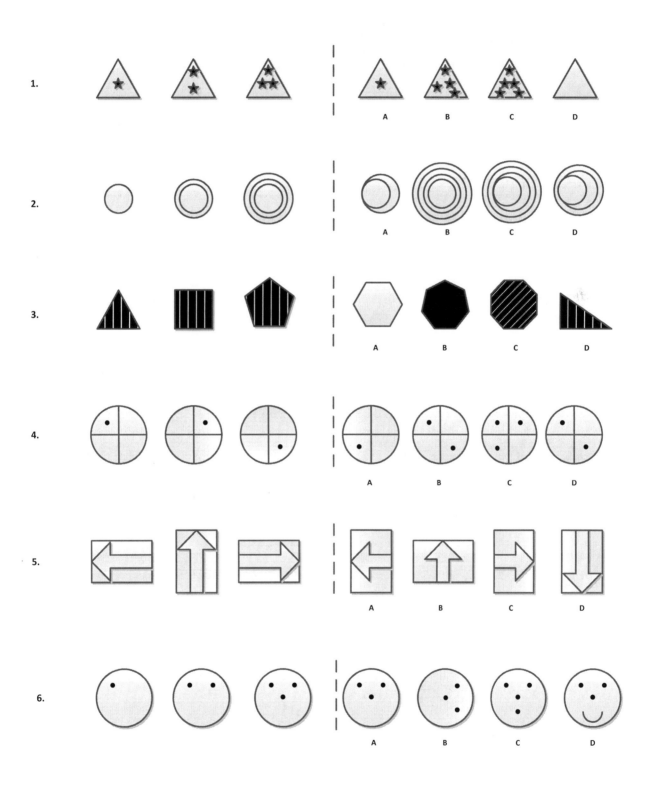

1.

2.

3.

4.

5.

6.

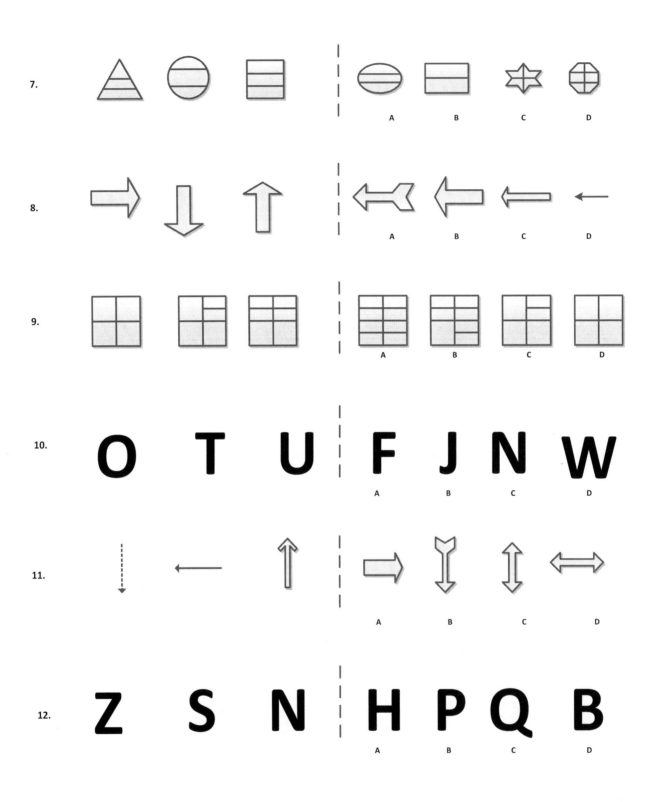

7.

8.

9.

10.

11.

12.

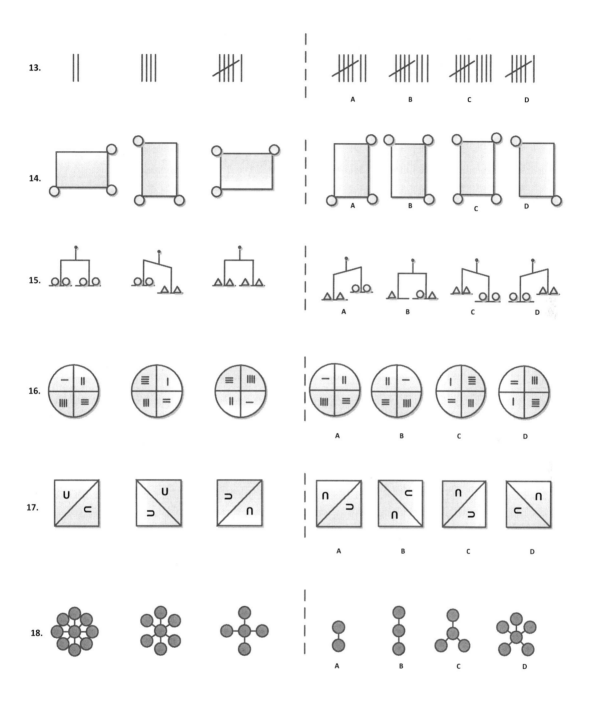

13.

14.

15.

16.

17.

18.

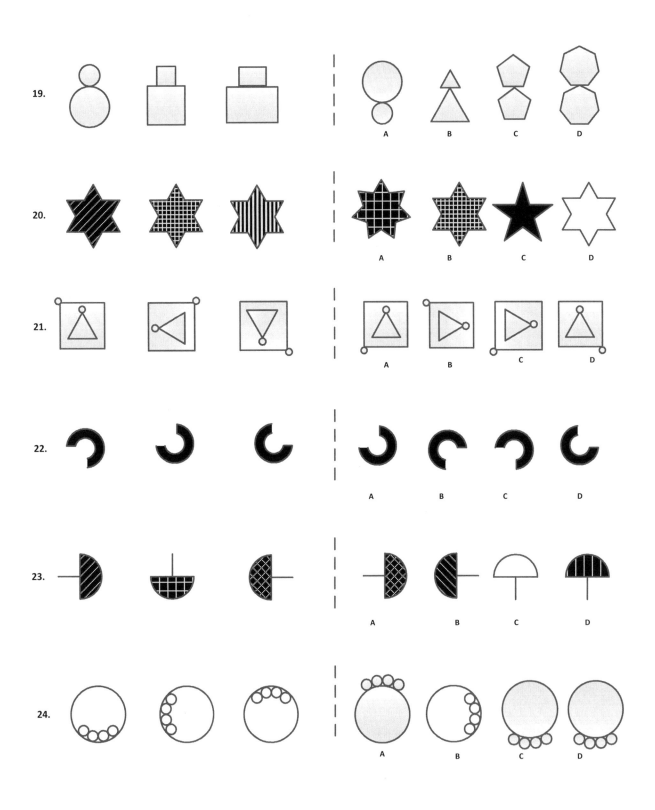

25.

Section 8: Figure Analogies

Instructions:

Here is a sample question in this section:

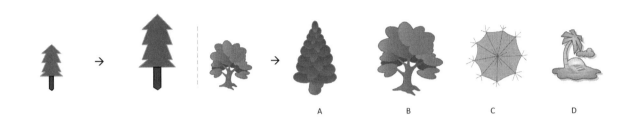

See the first two figures and figure out the relationship between these figures. Then see the third figure and the see the figure options A through D. See which option would be most applicable to relationship you found earlier. On the blank answer sheet at the end of this book, pencil in the bubble to answer the question.

Here option B is the answer. The relationship between first and second figure is that it has grown in size. Option B is the grown form of the third figure.

All the questions in this section can be solved in the same manner.

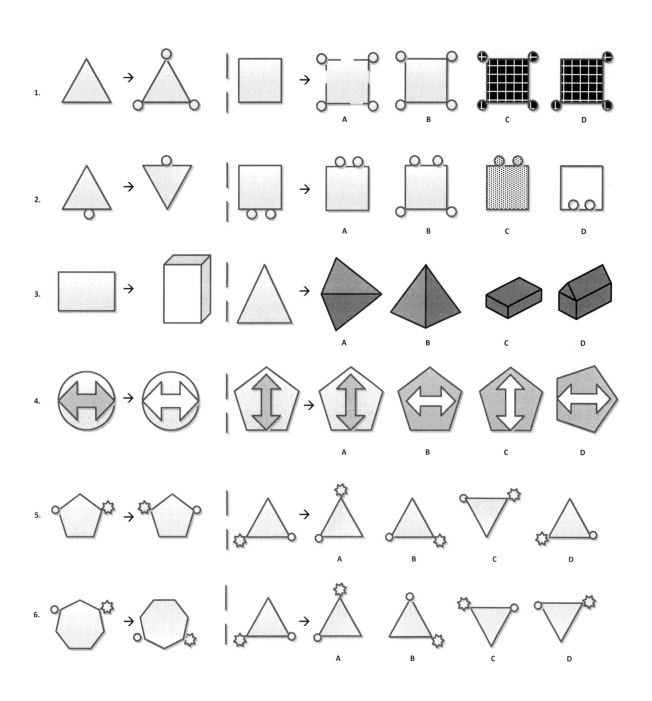

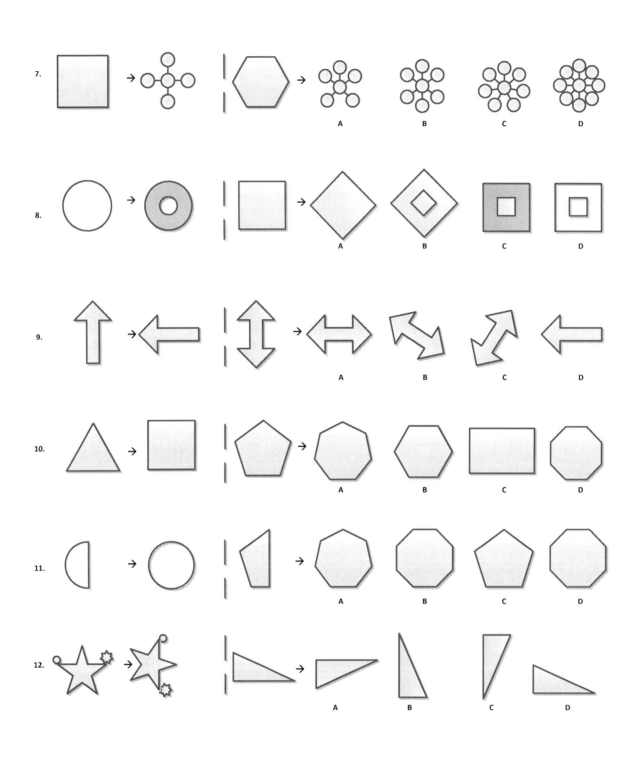

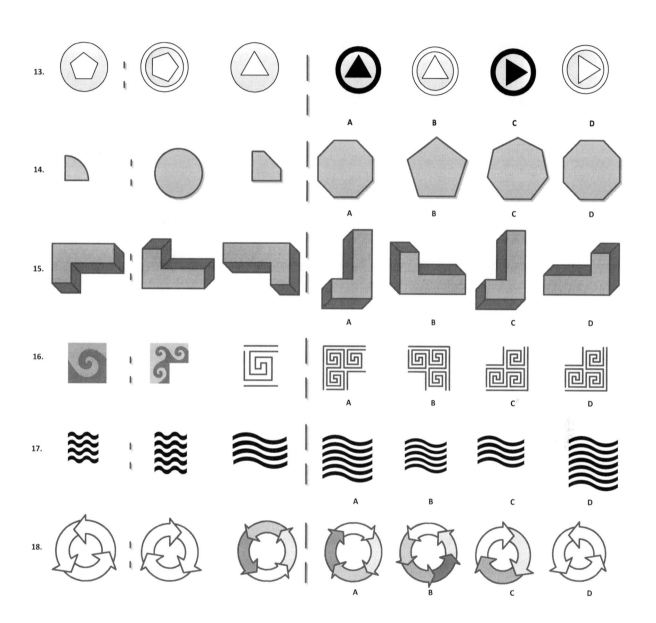

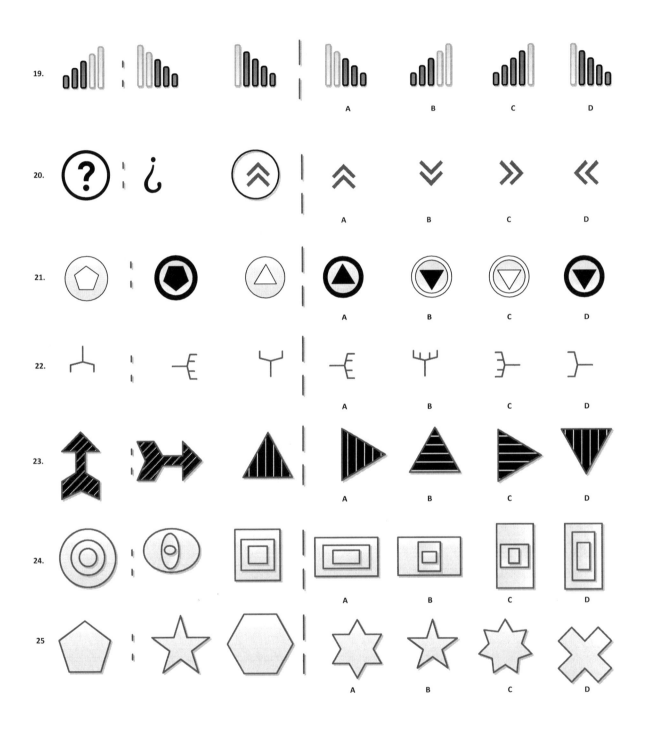

Section 9: Figure Analysis

Instructions:

Here is a sample question in this section:

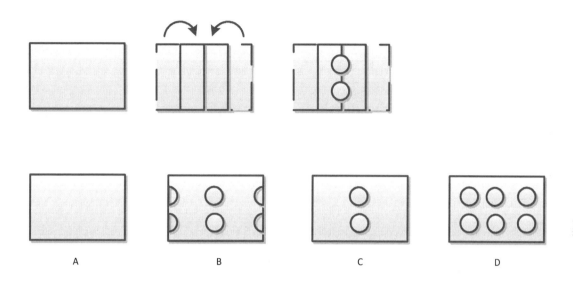

A	B	C	D

See the first three figures and how the page is folded. The last figure in the 1st row tells you how and where a hole is punched in the figure. Then see the options A through D. Then see how when the paper is unfolded after the hole is punched. What will the paper look like? It should match one of the options given here. On the blank answer sheet at the end of this book, pencil in the bubble to answer the question.

Here option B is the answer. When you open up the folds, the paper should like option B.

All the questions in this section can be solved in the same manner.

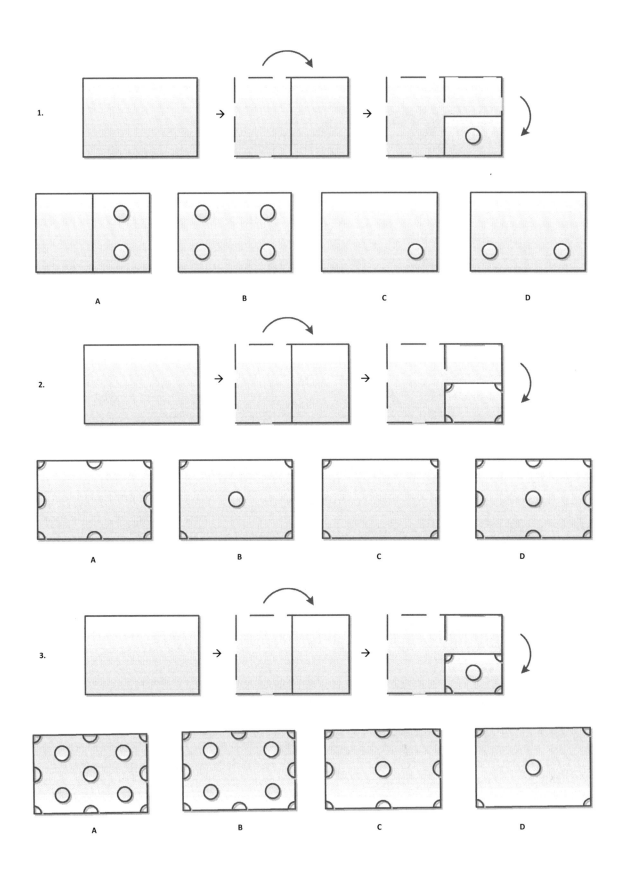

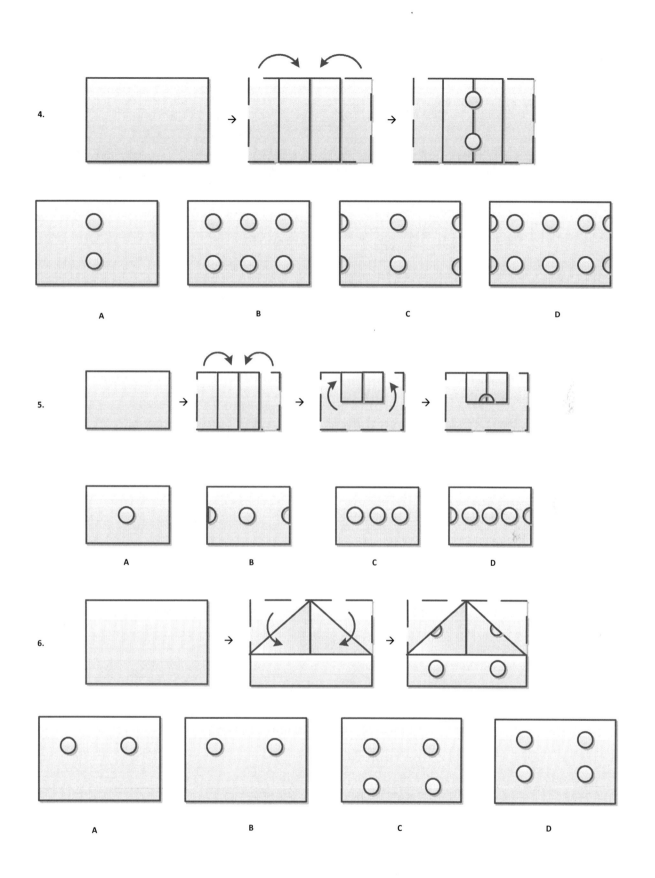

4.

A   B   C   D

5.

A   B   C   D

6.

A   B   C   D

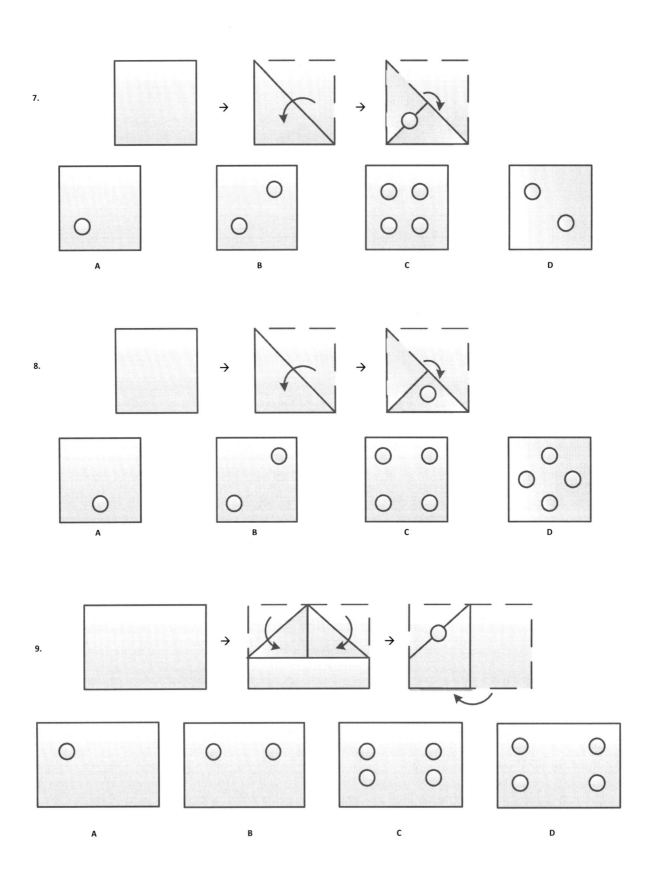

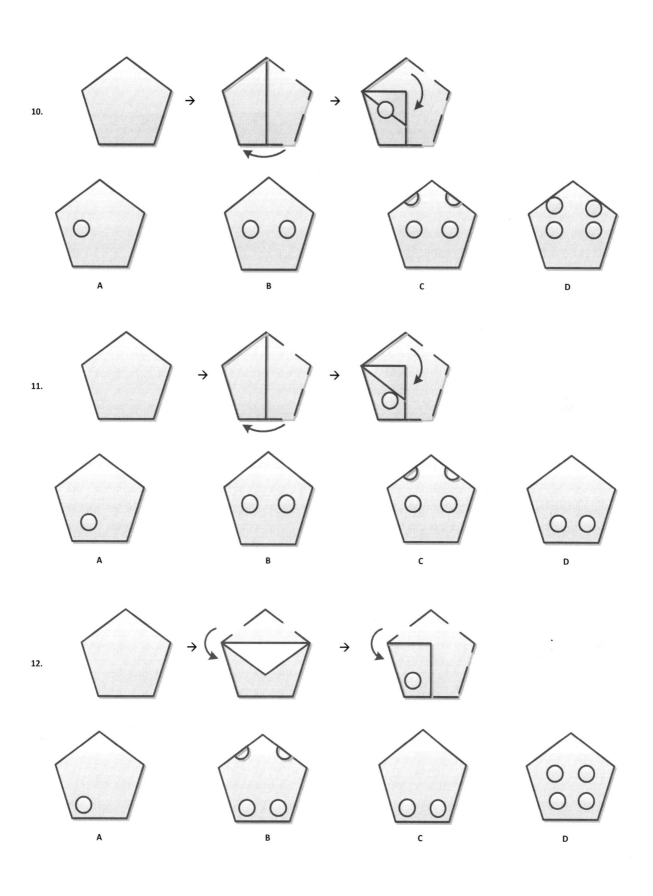

10.

A   B   C   D

11.

A   B   C   D

12.

A   B   C   D

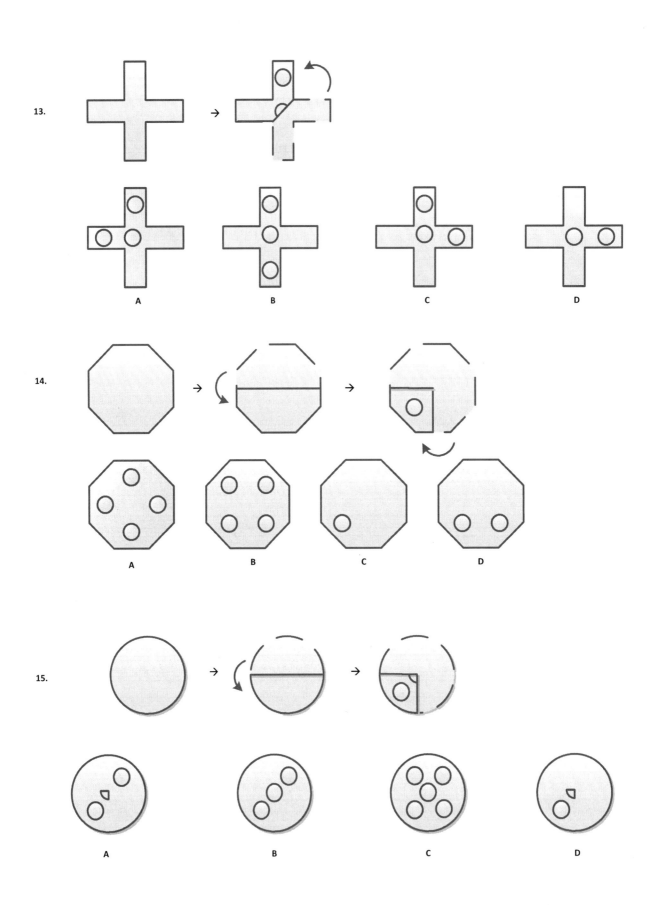

Name: _____   Date: _____

Section 7: Figure Classification	Section 8: Figure Analogies	Section 9: Figure Analysis
1 A B C D	1 A B C D	1 A B C D
2 A B C D	2 A B C D	2 A B C D
3 A B C D	3 A B C D	3 A B C D
4 A B C D	4 A B C D	4 A B C D
5 A B C D	5 A B C D	5 A B C D
6 A B C D	6 A B C D	6 A B C D
7 A B C D	7 A B C D	7 A B C D
8 A B C D	8 A B C D	8 A B C D
9 A B C D	9 A B C D	9 A B C D
10 A B C D	10 A B C D	10 A B C D
11 A B C D	11 A B C D	11 A B C D
12 A B C D	12 A B C D	12 A B C D
13 A B C D	13 A B C D	13 A B C D
14 A B C D	14 A B C D	14 A B C D
15 A B C D	15 A B C D	15 A B C D
16 A B C D	16 A B C D	
17 A B C D	17 A B C D	
18 A B C D	18 A B C D	
19 A B C D	19 A B C D	
20 A B C D	20 A B C D	
21 A B C D	21 A B C D	
22 A B C D	22 A B C D	
23 A B C D	23 A B C D	
24 A B C D	24 A B C D	
25 A B C D	25 A B C D	

Answer Key

Section 1: Verbal Classification	Section 2: Sentence Completion	Section 3: Verbal Analogies
1. C	1. A	1. B
2. B	2. B	2. A
3. D	3. A	3. A
4. B	4. B	4. B
5. A	5. B	5. C
6. A	6. C	6. A
7. C	7. D	7. C
8. C	8. A	8. B
9. D	9. D	9. D
10. A	10. B	10. A
11. B	11. A	11. A
12. A	12. C	12. B
13. B	13. C	13. A
14. C	14. B	14. B
15. A	15. A	15. A
16. B	16. A	16. B
17. C	17. B	17. A
18. C	18. A	18. A
19. A	19. B	19. B
20. D	20. D	20. D
		21. A
		22. C
		23. D
		24. A
		25. A

Section 4: Quantitative Relations	Section 5: Number Series	Section 6: Equation Building
		1. B
1. C	1. B	2. C
2. C	2. C	3. A
3. A	3. A	4. A
4. B	4. C	5. A
5. A	5. A	6. B
6. B	6. B	7. B
7. A	7. A	8. C
8. B	8. B	9. A
9. A	9. A	10. D
10. B	10. B	11. B
11. B	11. C	12. A
12. C	12. A	13. B
13. A	13. D	14. D
14. A	14. B	15. C
15. B	15. C	
16. A	16. A	
17. A	17. A	
18. C	18. D	
19. C	19. A	
20. B	20. A	
21. A		
22. A		
23. C		
24. B		
25. C		

Section 7: Figure Classification	Section 8: Figure Analogies	Section 9: Figure Analysis
1. B	1. B	1. B
2. B	2. A	2. D
3. D	3. A	3. A
4. A	4. C	4. C
5. D	5. B	5. B
6. C	6. C	6. C
7. A	7. B	7. B
8. B	8. C	8. D
9. B	9. A	9. B
10. D	10. B	10. C
11. A	11. C	11. D
12. A	12. C	12. C
13. B	13. D	13. C
14. B	14. D	14. B
15. A	15. D	15. C
16. D	16. A	
17. B	17. B	
18. B	18. A	
19. B	19. C	
20. B	20. B	
21. C	21. D	
22. B	22. C	
23. D	23. A	
24. B	24. B	
25. D	25. A	

Made in the USA
San Bernardino, CA
28 October 2013